W9-CGM-275

The founding of St. Olaf was a distinct venture by an immigrant group only recently settled on the frontier in south central Minnesota. It was an act of faith by which the Norse immigrant hoped to make his life in America more secure. Transferred into a strangely different environment, the character of the Norse pioneer became a part of the very foundations of American life and culture in the upper midwest.

From *High on Manitou* by William C. Benson, 1949

*The view from the hill is very extensive and exhibits of the
most pleasing panoramas to be found in Minnesota.*

From *Quarter Centennial Souvenir of St. Olaf College*, 1899

Music ensembles at Boe Memorial Chapel

St. Olaf in Minnesota is an exceptional place, and with Wooster, one of the two best-kept secrets in higher education simply because it has never made an effort to attract a nationwide applicant pool rather than a predominantly Midwest Lutheran one. Its faculty is superb; indeed, its math department is as good as any in the country, even Dartmouth's. Its choir is famous, its kids are the kind you'd like yours to be. Out of curiosity I went to church on a visit there, and out of a student population of three thousand, there must have been a thousand at the service.

Loren Pope, in *Looking Beyond the Ivy League*

ST. OLAF
COLLEGE

PHOTOGRAPHED BY MITCH KEZAR
Black Star

Harmony House
Publishers Louisville

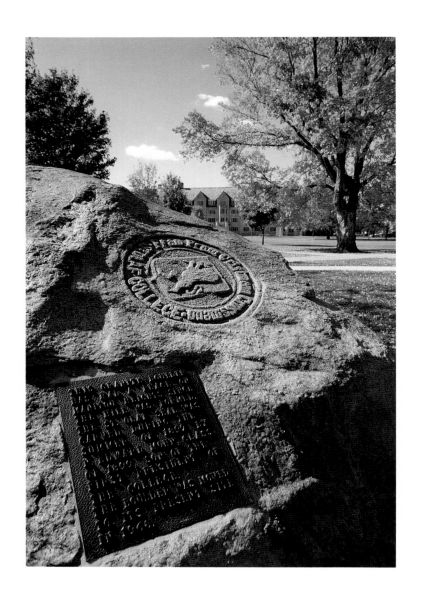

Executive Editors: William Butler and William Strode
Library of Congress Catalog Number: 90-81401
Hardcover International Standard Book Number 0-9l6509-74-5
Printed by Friesen Printers, Manitoba, Canada
First Edition printed Fall, 1990 by Harmony House Publishers,
P.O. Box 90, Prospect, Kentucky 40059 (502) 228-2010 / 228-4446
Copyright © 1990 by Harmony House Publishers
Photographs copyright © 1990 by Mitch Kezar

This book or portions thereof may not be reproduced in any form without
permission of Harmony House Publishers. Photographs may not be
reproduced in any form without permission of Mitch Kezar.

Boe Memorial Chapel

PREFACE

Whenever I speak with alumni of St. Olaf College, I am struck by their loyalty to and pride in this institution. Whether we are among those who have studied here or those who have become adopted Oles through the good fortune of our employment or marriage, we all cherish this community of faith and learning.

The genius of the St. Olaf community has been to remember and honor the traditions of the college while looking ahead to the future and the kind of world for which St. Olaf must prepare the young men and women who are its students. This is an institution that treasures its roots while living confidently and hopefully in the present and in the future.

St. Olaf has always put the student first, seeking to prepare that student for life, rather than for just a livelihood. We do that through an education which is committed to the liberal arts, is rooted in the Christian gospel, and incorporates a global perspective. That statement of mission is entirely in accord with the high standards of faith and learning set by its founders and developed and strengthened through the great men and women who have served St. Olaf for more than 100 years.

This pictorial view of St. Olaf is intended to help all of us who love this college be reminded of and inspired by its past and present in order that we many more effectively help St. Olaf carry out its mission in the future. The college's proud history has provided a foundation for the leadership role St. Olaf will continue to take in the century ahead, as it serves as a springboard from which new generations of wise and thoughtful graduates will embark upon their journey in the world. St. Olaf was established by its founders in an act of faith so that the children of immigrants could not only make their lives in America more secure but could also be of benefit to generations still to come. In that spirit, St. Olaf looks to the future — as a servant to society, the church and the world.

Melvin D. George
President

Holland Hall

INTRODUCTION

It was a cold night in early April, 1990 when a goodly number of St. Olaf faculty, emeriti, students and friends from the community met in the "Hauge Room" of Rolvaag Memorial Library to hear a presentation by a young assistant professor of Religion, who had been selected by his faculty colleagues to deliver the second of the Eighth Annual Carl A. Mellby Memorial Lectures.

He was there not to lecture, but to enter into serious dialogue with his colleagues, students and the community for he sees the current encounter of the world's religions as "one of the major challenges of our times."

Isn't this like St. Olaf; to face the challenge of the times? Does not the panorama of its brief history point to a succession of similar instances? This pictorial record of the institution sets before us memorials, as it were, on the landscape that is Manitou Heights. Many bear names — names that are reminiscent of some of the college's best moments. Not unlike Joshua, the Israelite leader who succeeded Moses, our forebears laid up these stones as memorials among us, that when our children ask, "What mean these stones?" we can tell them One speaks the names and the names tell of persons who had ideas, dreams, visions; all of which inspired the unfolding action that is the history of the college.

Is this so different from what the little group of Norwegian farmers, business people and pastors were about when they said 116 years earlier, "Let us teach our children this new language and the ways of this democratic society in the context of "the faith?" The professor made it very clear that he was speaking out of a deep appreciation of the faith commitment of St. Olaf and its people. Likewise he acknowledged a common commitment to the college's educational goals in its pursuit of truth.

The meeting to which reference was made at the outset was in the "Hauge Room" of the library. The room was named for a young man back in Norway who had inspired a movement, particularly among the laity in the church, and one of the persons touched by that movement was Bernt Julius Muus; the man whose resulting independence of spirit led him, with others of similar spirit to found St. Olaf's School.

Rolvaag Memorial Library where the meeting was held reminds one of a young lad from a fishing village on an island in Northern Norway who dreamed of one day becoming a professor in America. More than that, he became one of America's outstanding men of letters. He, too, was criticized by many because of the honest and open way he depicted life and trials of the immigrants on the American scene. Yet he established a basic principle in the liberal arts of looking to the poet, the dramatist and the novelist as the interpretors of life; for, as he put it, "Their senses are keener than mine. They have strained their vision; they have laid their ear close to the aching heart of humanity and listened long and breathlessly."

In a similar vein the study of history is remembered many in the vision of an Agnes Larson, her head tilted heavenward and her eyes closed, as she launched into a rhapsodic description of the renaissance period of European history. And not a few will recall how their childhood faith was recovered and legitimized through edifying classroom lectures and discussions under the late Harold Ditmanson's tutelage. With his vision of the creative tension between faith and learning he left this unforgettable quote: "The status quo at St. Olaf is always in motion, and therein lies our hope."

Not only the humanities but the sciences, as well, are affirmed in the names paraded before us. Emil O. Ellingson, the first St. Olaf graduate to receive a Ph.D. in chemistry came back to assist in laying the foundation for what has become one of the most prestigious undergraduate departments in the country, demonstrating the pursuit of scientific truth as a calling under God.

In the fine arts, F. Melius Christiansen found his way from Norway to become director of music at the young struggling school where he developed a choral program that would revolutionize vocal music in churches and schools throughout the land. So unusual was his work that a stunned New York critic was given to report on a choir concert in 1920, "Last night in the Metropolitan Opera House a group of 60 young men and women from the small towns and villages of the Midwest put on immortality for two hours." A decade or so later President Boe called a young St. Olaf graduate out of the pastoral ministry to "Cultivate his artistic talent," which, the president said, "would be his real contribution to the church." Subsequently, Arnold Flaten became the "loving critic" of everything artistic that happened on and off campus and left the mark of his personal faith on young lives as well as on wooden beams in the radio building and on the stone lintels of the library.

Where does one stop as he or she looks at these stones and is reminded of the names they bear? Quite apart from the centrality of academics let another broad sphere of campus life, namely, the compassionate and concerned care of students, be symbolized by the 42-year tenure of Gertrude Hilleboe as Dean of Women. Presidents have barely been mentioned and one would do well to recall the names like Thorson, Ytterboe, Holland and Skoglund without whose financial prowess and undaunted determination the college would not have survived despite its high sense of calling.

Viewing this pictorial presentation of St. Olaf College brings to mind the words of President Granskou at the naming of the 75th Anniversary celebration, "An Adventure in Faith." He said, "Our founders dared to risk their present for our future." And the task has not changed.

— *Clifford Swanson*
Campus Pastor emeritus

A ST. OLAF CHRONOLOGY

1869 Pastor B.J. Muus begins Holden Academy in his parsonage at Holden Church, 23 miles southeast of Northfield. Historians believe it was the starting point for what eventually would become St. Olaf College.

1874 Articles of Incorporation for St. Olaf's School signed in Northfield, Minnesota.

1875 Formal opening of St. Olaf's School, Pastor Thorbjorn Nelson Mohn installed as first Principal. Opening day registration - 36 students. First teachers are Mohn, Lars S. Reque and Ella Fiske.

1876 Negotiations completed for the purchase of 30 acres on Manitou Heights at a price of $1,250.

1878 Dedication of Old Main held in connection with celebration of Founders Day. Ties with Lutheran Church affirmed through representation by Synod leaders at the dedication.

1887 The first issue of *The Manitou Messenger*, the student newspaper, published.

1887 Beginning of St. Olaf — Carlton athletic rivalry with a baseball game played in Northfield.

1889 Board of Trustees passes resolution to change name from St. Olaf's School to St. Olaf College. Articles of Incorporation are formally changed. Th. N. Mohn officially named President of the college.

1890 First debating society founded; beginning of outstanding St. Olaf forensics program. Delegates of the United Norwegian Lutheran Church recognized St. Olaf College as their "Institution." First three Bachelor of Arts Degrees conferred upon Anton Engebretson, Carl J. Rollefson, Anders O. Sandbo. St. Olaf College band organized by Engebret Lee, a student.

1892 First St. Olaf Alumni Club organized in Minneapolis; C.J. Rollefson, President; F. E. Erickson, Vice President; Clara Bjornstad, Corresponding Secretary.

1893 First woman graduate, Agnes Mellby. Delegates of the United Norwegian Lutheran Church of America give full and unqualified support to St. Olaf as a College of the Church, reaffirming St. Olaf's affiliation with the Lutheran Church from its founding day.

1899 United Norwegian Lutheran Church of America votes to reaffirm that St. Olaf College is the college of the Church at its annual convention in Minneapolis.

1899 Rev. John Nathan Kildahl succeeds Rev. Th. N. Mohn as president of St. Olaf College.

1900 Rev. B. J. Muus, considered the founder of St. Olaf College, dies at his daughter's home in Trondhjeim, Norway.

1903 F. Melius Christiansen named Director of Music at St. Olaf College. He also served as Band Director.

1906 Ole Edvart Rolvaag is appointed to the faculty where he spends the remainder of his career teaching a variety of subjects including Geometry, Physiology, Greek, Geography, Old Testament History, Norwegian and English. Emil O. Ellingson is hired to teach Chemistry and Science. Ellingson is the first St. Olaf graduate to receive a Ph.D. in Chemistry from the University of Wisconsin in 1912. Under Ellingson's leadership, St. Olaf becomes one of the foremost educators of chemists in the United States.

1909 St. Olaf's first Rhodes Scholar, Joseph Tetlie, graduates.

1910 - 1911 Academic honor system established, and continues to operate today.

1912 The first St. Olaf Christmas Festival held in Hoyme Chapel to celebrate the birth of Christ through the beauty of song.

1914 Rev. Lauritz A. Vigness installed as third President of St. Olaf College.

1915 St. Olaf College accepted for membership in North Central Association and Association of American Colleges.

1917 St. Olaf Academy, the high school wing of St. Olaf College, is discontinued. Red Wing Seminary agrees to absorb students from St. Olaf Academy and St. Olaf agrees to take college-age students from Red Wing Seminary and enroll them in the collegiate program. Red Wing Seminary votes to join the St. Olaf Alumni Association. Affiliation with Norwegian Lutheran Church in America took place. The church body was reorganized as the Evangelical Lutheran Church in 1946.

1918 Lars Wilhelm Boe becomes 4th President of St. Olaf College. Experiments begin in Physics Department which lead to establishment of WCAL Radio Station.

1920 St. Olaf Choir makes its first major national tour earning rave reviews for performances in East Coast concert halls.

1921 Presentation of the "Merchant of Venice," directed by Elizabeth Walsingham Kelsey, marks beginning of strong tradition in theater.

1924 Rolvaag's *Giants in the Earth* is published in Norwegian.

1939 Norwegian Crown Prince Olav and Princess Martha visit St. Olaf College. As King Olav V, he will visit again in 1968, 1975 and 1987.

1943 Clemens M. Granskou named 5th President of St. Olaf College.

1945 Betty Halvorson elected first woman student body president.

1946 St. Olaf becomes member of Evangelical Lutheran Church, the old Norwegian Luther Church in America.

1949 St. Olaf granted a chapter of Phi Beta Kappa, Delta of Minnesota.

1951 First college pastor, The Rev. H. B. Hanson, appointed; St. Olaf Student Congregation organized.

1959 St. Olaf helps establish Associated Colleges of the Midwest.

1960 St. Olaf reaffirms church affiliation with newly formed American Lutheran Church.

1963 Sidney A. Rand named 6th President of St. Olaf College. 4-1-4 calendar year adopted by the faculty. Put into effect in 1964-65 school year. St. Olaf becomes the 6th college in the nation to adopt this plan. St. Olaf accredited by National Council for Accreditation of Teacher Education.

1965 International Studies Program becomes part of total academic program.

1969 Opening of the Paracollege, an alternative path to the B.A. degree, stressing an individualized program.

1974 St. Olaf celebrates its Centennial.

1980 Harlan Foss named 7th President of St. Olaf College.

1985 Melvin D. George becomes St. Olaf College's 8th President.

1988 St. Olaf reaffirmed as a National College of the Church with the newly formed Evangelical Lutheran Church in America.

St. Olaf is special in the quality of its students and faculty. There's a unique commitment to quality education — a strong motivation for commitment to excellence. Because of the class size and the personal commitment on the part of the faculty, a unique bond forms between faculty and students, a real sense of comaraderie.

Wendell H. Arneson,
Professor of Art

Looking east from the Science Center　　29

I dare say that the bulk of the students who attended the institution during the first thirty years of its existence, when they think of St. Olaf College, invariably see in their mind's eye the picture of that building which for forty-six years has stood on the brow of Manitou Heights facing the sunrising, seemingly as a guard over the destinies of Northfield. As one approaches the Main Building from the east, these words of the poet come to one's mind:

> *This castle hath a pleasant seat;*
> *the air*
> *Nimbly and sweetly recommends*
> *itself*
> *Unto our gentle senses.*

From *Fifty Years at St. Olaf* by Professor I.F. Grose

The Fireside Lounge

Fram, Fram, Christmenn, Crossmen. If we are true to this motto everything we do at St. Olaf will have meaning and purpose. A Christian college must be more than a training center. In its simplest language, it must be a community of inspired men and women who are bent on carrying out a program for the redemption of the world.

President Clemens Granskou

Across the Cannon River

The city of Northfield, lying in the pleasant Cannon Valley, amidst rolling country and surrounded by wooded hills, seems more like some New England city, the result of a century's slow growth and improvement, than a western town, sprung up within the memory of men still living; still, western push and energy are not lacking; the wide and well kept streets, the beautiful parks and squares, the stores and business blocks, the neat and pleasant residence portion — these are the evidences of enterprise and thrift which have made Northfield one of the finest cities of its size in the northwest.

From *Quarter Centennial Souvenir of St. Olaf College*, 1899

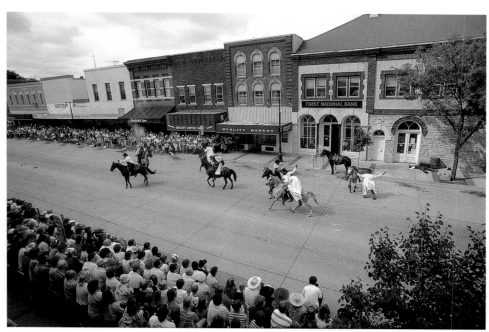

Jesse James Raid Reenactment

Alumni Days

I often receive comments from people who have met St. Olaf students. They tell me about how impressed they are by these young people, and their obvious sense of caring and their desire to make a contribution in life. Such comments confirm my conviction that St. Olaf is a college where the whole person — mind, body and spirit — can develop in new and energizing ways.

President Melvin D. George

Here dwells the thinker and the scholar, the poet and the missionary, the prophet and the reformer; all those who have a vision of a better world and have dedicated their abilities to its realization.

Dr. C.A. Mellby

Edna and Howard Hong in the Kierkegaard Library

Added to all this is some kind of St. Olaf "mystique," which means enough to many graduates to point to the existence of an esprit de corps supported by affinity and affection, shared experiences and common values.

From *Identity and Mission in a Changing Context,* 1974

Boe Chapel

While certainly St. Olaf must continue to improve its educational offering and strengthen its educational philosophy, I firmly believe that its commitment to the liberal arts in a Christian framework and with a global perspective is absolutely the right approach.

President Melvin D. George

Kelsey Theater

The Tormodsgaard-Bakken Recital Hall

Because life is more than a livlihood, a liberal education develops an understanding of an entire range of human achievement and focuses on what is ultimately worthwhile rather than on what is immediately useful. In so doing, it provides a sound foundation for the professional education and technical training which modern society requires.

From the *College Catalog*

Larson Hall

The handbell choir at the Christmas Festival Smorgasbord

After the Christmas Festival concert

Kenneth Jennings conducting The St. Olaf Christmas Festival Concert

We shall all be glad to get home and give you a concert on the hill. As great as it is to be greeted by thousands of people at the concerts, it is nothing quite so great as to sing for our own faculty and students at St. Olaf.

Letter from Professor F. Melius Christiansen to President Boe

One of the ten Christmas events in the U.S. not to be missed.

From *The New York Times*

For a college to preserve and impart a genius of its own will be, fearfully, a very radical idea in the future. There is a danger that no more than a core corps of private colleges may survive as exceptions.

Pray God the second line will be here on Manitou Heights in 2074, praising the Lord and serving truth with a distinction equal to the first line which you represent today.

Father Colman J. Barry, O.S.B., in his centennial commencement address, 1974

Final instructions in Boe Chapel

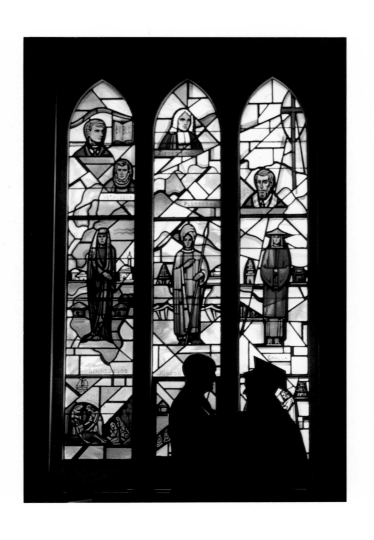

Baccalaureate Service

Graduation Day at Manitou Field

A LOOK BACK AT ST. OLAF
in photographs from the archives

Old Main, January 21, 1888

The University's first Board of Trustees, July, 1886. The Rev. Bernt Julius Muus, recognized as the founder of St. Olaf, is seated to the right of the flower stand. The Rev. Thorbjorn Mohn, first president of St. Olaf, is seated behind and to right of Muus. Dr. John Kildahl, who succeeded Mohn in 1899, stands behind Muus.

June 22, 1918. The Committee on Location of Buildings does its work on the lawn in front of Main.

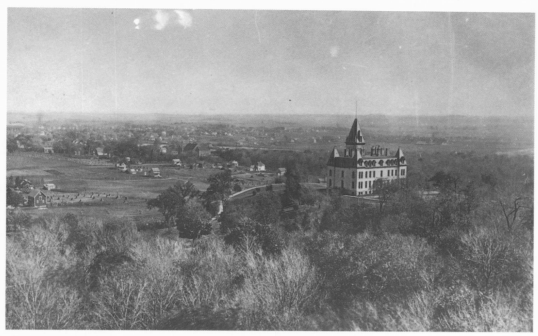

Old Main, October 16, 1900.

The cornerstone-laying of the Steensland Library, 1902.

The construction of Ytterboe Hall, September, 1900.

An April, 1888 view of the Cannon River and the town of Northfield.

Main, Library and Chapel, March 9, 1916.

Hoyme Memorial Chapel fire, September 22, 1923.

This barn, shown here in September, 1906, was constructed on the present site of the St. Olaf Center.

Agnes Mellby is in charge of the Steensland Libary in this February, 1907 photograph.

H.A. Boe and O. A. Lysne sit in a buggy under the stained glass window in Hoyme Chapel, July 24, 1916.

The Senior/Junior Reception, 1898,
with Ladies Hall in the background

March, 1879. The first student/faculty group to occupy Old Main.
The building was first used in the fall of 1878.

Women students at Ladies Hall, April, 1911.

The first class at St. Olaf, in the first school building at 3rd and Union in Northfield, March, 1875.

Crown Prince Olav of Norway and President Boe, May, 1939.

College students gather at Old Main in 1907.

Three St. Olaf presidents — Kildahl, Vigness and Boe — stand with a portrait of a fourth, President Mohn, September, 1918.

Old Main, July 14, 1886.

May 28, 1888. Ladies play croquet in front of Ladies Hall.

Ladies Hall in the winter of 1886.

The St. Olaf faculty, June, 1904.

The Dining Hall in the basement of Old Main, November, 1887.

Students in Chapel, February, 1907.

The St. Olaf Band in front of the Steensland Library, 1903.

The first college class, June 17, 1890. The three men are Carl J. Rollefson, Anders Oswald Sandbo, and Anton Engebretson.

St. Olaf College Band, 1901.

The Band in 1895.

The College Choir, 1911.

Homecoming, 1926.

Christmas pageant, 1940.

A class in the Norwegian-American room of the Rolvaag Library in 1947.
That's Profesor Theodore Jorgenson presiding.

The St. Olaf football squad, 1904.

St. Olaf vs. Carleton, November 5, 1921.

Dedication Day at the Anders Haugen Ski Slide, January 13, 1913.

Football star Ole Gunderson in 1971.

Women's track, 1920, with Mohn Hall in the background.

A basketball game in 1922.

Women's Phys Ed class in the new gym, 1920.

The basketball team, 1912-13.

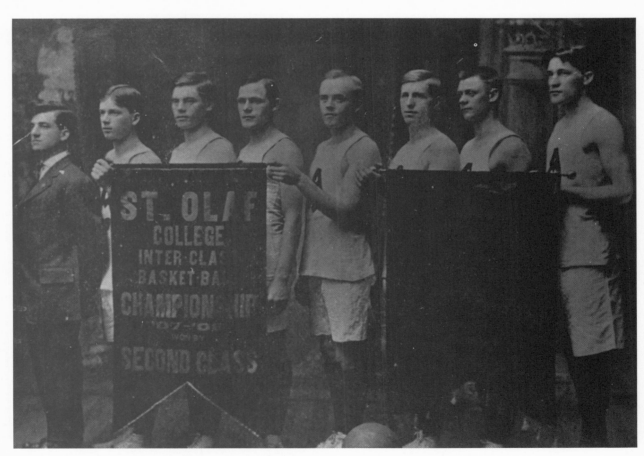

The basketball team, winners of the Inter-Class basketball championship, 1907-1908.

A June, 1888 croquet match in front of Ladies Hall.

Men's Phys Ed, ca. 1920.

Track and field event, 1920.

St. Olaf's first baseball game, vs. Carleton, May 14, 1887.

Air Force ROTC in the early 1960s.

President Granskou greeting President Eisenhower, 1952.

Homecoming parade, 1947.

Military training, 1918.

The St. Olaf Student Army Training Corps, November 11, 1918.

Vice President Hubert Humphrey visits campus, 1965.

Coretta Scott King at St. Olaf.

Crown Princess Astrid of Norway on campus in the spring of 1958.

The mission of St. Olaf College is to provide a liberal arts education rooted in the Christian gospel and incorporating a global perspective. In its educational program, the college seeks to foster the development of the whole person in mind, body, and spirit.

St. Olaf College Mission Statement